DARLINGTON
A Pictorial History

St Cuthbert's Church, Darlington

DARLINGTON
A Pictorial History

Robert Woodhouse

Phillimore

1998

Published by
PHILLIMORE & CO. LTD.
Shopwyke Manor Barn, Chichester, West Sussex

ISBN 1 86077 085 1

Printed and bound in Great Britain by
BIDDLES LTD.
Guildford, Surrey

List of Illustrations

Frontispiece: St Cuthbert's Church, Darlington

1. Unveiling of South African War Memorial, 5 August 1905
2. Flock of geese at the entrance to St Cuthbert's churchyard
3. Official reception for troops from the Boer War in 1901
4. *Boot and Shoe Hotel* and market place
5. View of the market place
6. Monday market in 1950
7. Horse market in the 1930s
8. Aerial view of Darlington market in the 1930s
9. Rooftop view of central Darlington High Row
10. Northern end of High Row in the early 1900s
11. View along High Row in the early 1900s
12. View from High Row into Northgate in the early 1900s
13. Pease statue and entrance to Bondgate from High Row
14. View along High Row, 1920
15. Northern end of High Row, *c.*1880
16. Cattle market on west side of High Row
17. Celebrations on High Row
18. Pease statue and *King's Head Hotel*
19. Midland Bank, *King's Head Hotel* and Monument Rooms
20. New *King's Head Hotel*
21. High Row, 1930
22. The perimeter of the market place, 1910
23. Prebend Row in about 1890
24. Tubwell Row
25. Tubwell Row, 1907
26. Tubwell Row, 1920
27. North side of Tubwell Row, 1959
28. *Nag's Head Inn*, 1916
29. Church Lane behind the *Nag's Head Inn*
30. Old Stone Bridge and Ropery Yard
31. Approach to Stone Bridge
32. Old Stone Bridge
33. Rooftop view of Darlington, 1938
34. Rooftop view of Darlington, 1940
35. Ink and water-colour illustration, 'In Bondgate—on a slide'
36. Bulmer's Stone, 1890
37. Bondgate in about 1890
38. Horse fair in Bondgate during 1890
39. Bondgate, 1930
40. Junction of Bull Wynd and Houndgate
41. Bondgate, 1920
42. Junction of Blackwellgate and Houndgate
43. Horse-drawn trams
44. Mechanics' Yard in the mid-1920s
45. Blackwellgate, 1907
46. Midday scene, 1908
47. Northgate, 1910
48. Northgate, 1910
49. Single decker trolley buses on Northgate
50. Northgate, 1930
51. Skinnergate, 1948
52. Victoria Road, 1929
53. Old railway 'cut' at eastern end of Parkgate
54. Eastward view along Victoria Road
55. Victoria Road, 1906
56. Victoria Road, 1920
57. Darlington park gates in 1906
58. North Lodge Park
59. Bandstand, lake and mock castle in North Lodge Park
60. Bandstand in North Lodge Park
61. River Skerne and South Park, 1905
62. Park House in South Park
63. John Fowler monument in South Park
64. Entrance to Southend Avenue
65. Ornate fountain with date '1866'
66. Cast-iron drinking fountain, Milbank Road
67. Bus shelter, Haughton Road
68. Victorian wrought-iron gate, Cleveland Terrace
69. Pierremont, home of Henry Pease
70. Mowden Hall
71. 'Woodlands', built by Robert Botcherby
72. Darlington Free Library, 1910
73. View of Pease's Mill and north side of Priestgate
74. Mechanics' Institute, Skinnergate
75. Grange Road Baptist Chapel
76. Bondgate Methodist Church
77. Liberal and Unionist Club
78. Grammar School, Vane Terrace
79. The Teacher Training College

80. The Teacher Training College
81. Gateway and clock tower, Pierremont estate
82. The New Hippodrome and Palace of Varieties, 1907
83. Members of Darlington Operatic Society
84. Staff at Robert Brown's provision stores
85. Staff of Gallon's Ltd. at Parkgate
86. Group of musicians in a Darlington yard
87. Members and officials of Darlington (Eastbourne) Allotments, Limited
88. North Eastern Railway paint shop staff, 1910
89. The Darlington and Teesdale Naturalist Field Club in South Park, 1919
90. Darlington Workpeople's Horse Ambulance
91. Detachment of Whessoe Ltd.'s Home Guard in the Second World War
92. Cartoon by George A. Fothergill
93. Shop fitting work by Messers Blackett & Son at 13a Bondgate
94. Hintons, Bondgate
95. 'Geordie' Fawbert, pictured outside his shop on Clay Row
96. Darlington Quoits Club members, 1860
97. St Paul's, Darlington football team photographed in 1903-4 season
98. Bill head of Thomas Morritt, publican of the *Three Tuns* and *Post Office Hotel*, 1860
99. Art deco frontage of S. Tetley & Sons Ltd.
100. Prize-winning Co-operative milk float
101. Vehicles outside the Model Dairy in Melland Street
102. Darlington Co-operative Society Bakery Department delivery van
103. Darlington Co-operative and Industrial Society, Priestgate
104. Frontage of Co-operative Society's self service store
105. Darlington Co-operative advertisement
106. Fox's oriental cafe and creamery
107. Darlington Forge
108. Massive forge hammer known as 'Tiny Tim'
109. Darlington Forge Company Band
110. Woodwork between the chancel arch at Barningham Church
111. Steel roadway bridge at Cleveland Bridge and Engineering
112. Bridge Yard at Cleveland Bridge and Engineering Company's Yard
113. Illustrating Friends' Sunday School Teachers' Conference, 1874
114. Ox roasting to mark the coronation of Edward VII, 1902
115. Party in Beaumont Street, July 1919
116. Black-faced sheep at Darlington Show, 1920
117. Shire horse 'Rand Footprint' in 1928
118. Group at the Grand Parade on Cooperation Day in July 1930
119. Delivery horse at Grand Parade on Co-operation Day
120. Visit of Princess Henry of Battenberg, 24 October 1905
121. Railway carnival float from 1930s
122. Carnival float from 1930s
123. Barmpton Hall
124. Ketton Hall
125. Colling Shorthorn Memorial Challenge Cup
126. Cockerton Bridge
127. Former *Punch Bowl Inn*, 1900
128. Former *Punch Bowl Inn*, 1987
129. Blackwell crossroads in early 1900s
130. Blackwell crossroads in early 1900s
131. Brougham carriage
132. Locomotion No.1 outside North Road Station
133. Time Bill of 1825 for SDR Company's coach, 'Experiment'
134. Advertisement for Stockton & Darlington Railway
135. Fares and times for SDR in 1840
136. Sketch of Locomotion No.1 on the opening day in 1825
137. Railway cavalcade crossing Skerne Bridge, 1825
138. SDR station buildings at Fighting Cocks
139. North Road Station
140. Railway Workmen's Institute
141. North Road Locomotive Works
142. North Road Locomotive Works
143. Railway accident at Darlington, 15 November 1910
144. North Road railway bridge
145. Wrecked carriages and signals after accident on 27 June 1928
146. Steam locomotive No.62768 ex LNER 4-4-0 Class D49
147. Opening of Darlington tramway system
148. Tramcars from Darlington Light Railways
149. Italian musicians outside Dinsdale Rectory
150. Children on their way to Dinsdale village school, 1910
151. Fishlocks Mill on river Tees at Low Dinsdale
152. Dinsdale Weir and Fishlocks Mill in about 1890
153. Ladies near Dinsdale weir and fishlocks in the 1890s
154. The ruined chapel at Sockburn, exterior
155. The ruined chapel at Sockburn, interior
156. Effigies at the ruined chapel at Sockburn
157. Cardwell family on the frozen river Tees at Low Coniscliffe, January 1940
158. Piercebridge village green in about 1905
159. High Coniscliffe in about 1900
160. Cockerton village
161. Aycliffe village
162. *Old Scotch Corner Inn*, 1934
163. Fighting Cocks in parish of Middleton St George
164. Croft Bridge

165. River in flood at Croft Bridge
166. Illustration 'On Croft Bridge 1816'
167. Riverside property at Croft, 1909
168. Milbanke pew at Croft Church
169. Croft Spa in early 1900s
170. Middleton One Row, 1913

171. *Dinsdale Spa Hotel*
172. Family groups on riverside near Middleton One Row
173. Coat of arms for Darlington
174. Quaker burial ground behind the Friends' Meeting House in Skinnergate

Acknowledgements

I am greatly indebted to a number of people for their assistance with many aspects of this book.

Staff in Darlington Library's Centre for Local Studies have dealt with individual questions and queries as they have arisen and directed me to a whole range of materials about the town and neighbourhood.

Alan Suddes, curator of Darlington Museum, has provided a tremendous amount of support, advice and accurate information. His enthusiasm and wide ranging knowledge have played a major part in the completion of this work and I am most appreciative of his efforts.

In addition to postcards from my own local collection, items have been included from several other sources. These include a number of previously unpublished photographs from the archives of Darlington Museum Service and other materials from the Beamish Regional Resource Centre Photographic Library. Again, I am most grateful to Jim Lawson and other members of the staff at Beamish for their unstinting support and co-operation. Material for the endpapers has been selected from *Darlington 100 Years Ago*, 1906.

Illustration acknowledgements: Beamish Regional Resource Centre, 2, 4-5, 7-9, 12-27, 33, 35-6, 38-9, 42-3, 45-52, 54-6, 60-74, 76, 78-86, 88, 90, 92-105, 107-8, 111-113, 115-26, 131, 136-7, 139-145, 147-51, 159-61, 163, 166-167, 170, 173; S. Cardwell, 6, 28-32, 34, 37, 40-1, 44, 53, 77, 89, 127, 157, 162; G. Coates, 75, 128, 158; D. Morrell, 1, 87, 91, 109, 114, 132-35, 138; *The Northern Echo*, 129, 148; T. Wicken, 146; R. Woodhouse, 10, 11, 57-9, 152-6, 164-5, 168-9, 171-2.

Introduction

There is little documentary evidence about Darlington's early history but its geographical position accounts for the town's subsequent development as a market centre. Situated at the intersection of several trade routes beside the lowest crossing point of the Skerne, before its confluence with the River Tees—some five kilometres away to the south—it would serve a large agricultural hinterland on all sides.

Variations in the course of the River Skerne and recurring floods would probably rule out early settlement but recent excavations and test pits during improvement work along the river point to clearance of woodland for agriculture in the area towards the end of the fifth century B.C. Other clearance work seems to have taken place during the early and late Bronze Age. By the beginning of the Iron Age, cereals were under widespread cultivation in the area and recent aerial surveys have identified a large settlement west of Neasham.

During the Roman period, major river crossings were established on the Tees at Piercebridge and Middleton St George but there is no firm evidence of Romano-British occupation at Darlington. The first documentary reference to Darlington appears in an 11th-century Land Grant as 'Dearthingtun' and during the following century mention was made of 'Dearnington'. Experts suggest that 'Derring' was the Anglian name for the River Skerne and in 1876 an Anglian cemetery site was uncovered on the Greenbank estate. Six graves dating from the sixth and seventh centuries contained large numbers of artefacts but, although they were identified as 'pagan' graves, their positioning in the traditional Christian east-west alignment may show that they belong to a period in the seventh century when Christianity was spread through the north of England by Edwin of Northumbria and Paulinus.

No evidence has been found of an adjacent Anglian settlement but the cemetery included at least one child and it seems likely that there was a sizeable township in the vicinity. By the late 10th century the settlement at Darlington had gained considerable importance and a land grant by Styr, son of Ulphus to St Cuthbert in the early 11th century contained a reference to 'Darlington and its dependencies'.

Speculation about a Saxon church in Darlington focuses on the discovery of masonry from a pre-12th-century building and fragments of ninth- or 10th-century crosses during restoration of the existing church of St Cuthbert in 1865. It seems likely that, if such a church existed, it was sited further west from the present building—within the area now covered by the market place.

Work on the parish church of St Cuthbert probably started in the early 1190s on the orders of the Bishop of Durham, Hugh de Puiset. He conceived it as the grand church of his important manor of Darlington—a collegiate church with a dean and four canons—and may have used some of the money obtained from his tenants and bondsmen to pay the ransom for King Richard I. The fabric is well preserved and, in spite of the addition of the arcaded belfry and ribbed spire in the late 14th century and restoration work during the 19th century, it is virtually all in one style.

Regarded as one of the most important Early English churches in the north of England, the grand plan has a crossing tower and chancel, transepts and nave of equal height. The stately west front has two storeys of lancets and blind arcading, while the lofty nave features alternating round and clustered columns and transepts that repeat the theme of lancets and blind arcades. The chancel is of similar height and is divided from the rest of the building by a stone screen or pulpitum.

The interior has many fine features including 18 chancel stalls of black oak. Given to the church by Bishop Langley in the early 15th century, their traceried bench-ends have poppyheads with carved seraphim and human faces, and buttresses of lions, birds and prim little angels. A Victorian mosaic reredos depicting the Last Supper—the work of John Dobbin—was designed for Westminster Abbey but rejected by the Dean. In the south transept is a medieval font with a towering Restoration canopy and in a recess of the north transept is a red stone Norman sundial which was found during maintenance work in 1865. Among many tablets in the transepts, several feature the Havelock-Allan family—most notably General Sir Henry Havelock-Allan, the hero of Lucknow.

In 1183 Bishop Puiset commissioned an account, settlement by settlement, of his tenant's obligations—both individual and collective—and the findings are recorded in the Boldon Book. The survey describes Darlington as a prosperous town with a mixture of bonded villeins (probably based in the Bondgate area of the town) and leaseholders who were excused from serving on the Bishop's mission. It seems that the local community reared cattle and hens and were involved in cloth dyeing—with a watermill and smithy playing vital roles in the local economy.

The Bishop's manor house was probably built in the 1160s on a site to the south of the churchyard that later became the Duke of Cleveland's Leadyard. During the 18th century it operated as a workhouse and in 1870 the house and grounds were sold to Richard Luck for £2,000. Demolition followed in 1820 and several houses, known as Luck's Terrace and Luck's Square, were built on the site. These, in turn, were removed to make way for the new Town Hall.

The Deanery stood at the north-west corner of Feethams and the Horsemarket—fronting on to the market place. In 1875 it was purchased by the Corporation from the Duke of Cleveland and, in accordance with the terms of the sale, it was demolished during the following year.

The origins of a market are unclear but, by the mid-13th century, Darlington market and annual fairs attracted large numbers of people from most sectors of the north east.

The household books of the convent of Durham, with early references dating from around 1250, show regular purchases from Darlington market. A survey of the Bishop's territory was made in 1380 and reported that ... 'for the toll of the market place and market of Darlyngton, with the profit of the mills at Darlyngton Black there is rendered four score and ten pounds.' By 1532 Monday was established as market day in the town and this arrangement continues today.

During the 17th century, and in the face of opposition from neighbouring settlements such as Durham and Richmond, local people set up a fortnightly cattle market. A whole range of measures was needed to cope with the large numbers of tradespeople and livestock that arrived for Darlington's markets. One regulation states that 'no traders were to fodder their horses in or against the towl boath' and another recorded that 'all who brought corn etc. to the market place and brought stones or sward to sit upon shall immediately return them to where they came or be fined one shilling'. From the early days of the market until 1854 it was the custom to have one or two men stationed at each entrance to the town to collect tolls and they had the power of seizure in cases of non-payment. It was also forbidden to avoid market tolls by selling in streets outside the market place. In 1658 one of the free burgesses of Richmond had a heifer seized in Darlington for refusing to pay the toll that had been demanded.

During Henry VIII's reign, Leland recorded that Darlington 'was the best market town in the bishoprick' and on 6 June 1752 it was stated that ... 'on the Monday had been held the greatest market for wool that had ever been known there ... £1,000 being laid out therein'.

Until the 19th century the market was administered by a bailiff appointed by the Bishop of Durham but in 1854 the local authority, under the Darlington Local Board Act, purchased the market rights for the sum of £7,854 19s. 4d.

By the late 14th century Darlington market was at the heart of increasing economic activity and, along with Stockton on Tees (some 12 miles away to the east), the town was already playing an important part in shipment of wool to the continent. Clearly-defined routes through the town had also been established by this time with streets such as Houndgate, Blackwellgate, Skinnergate and Northgate most prominent. A survey ordered by Bishop Hatfield in 1380 highlights the distinction between the Borough of Darlington, with its free tenants and burgesses, and nearby Bondgate where tenants held their land from the Bishop of Durham.

Continued economic prosperity during the 16th century saw the development of craft industries such as tanning and weaving alongside a thriving wool trade. In 1577 the town's first recorded guild—of shoemakers—was established but eight years later a major fire in the High Row and Skinnergate area caused widespread damage. About 300 houses were destroyed and, as a result, some 800 people were made homeless.

Darlington has a long tradition of academic institutions and it is possible that an early grammar school in the town was linked with the collegiate church of St Cuthbert. In about 1530 Robert Marshall is known to have established a grammar school building and chantry chapel but the location is not clear. The school premises may have been sited on land adjacent to the church overlooking the river Skerne.

Some 30 years later, in 1563, Queen Elizabeth I granted a charter for the establishment of a grammar school and buildings were erected on the churchyard site in 1647 and 1813. This 19th-century single-storey building was sited at the south-eastern end of the churchyard and an additional floor level was added in 1846.

Pupils moved to new premises on Vane Terrace in the mid-1870s and further building work took place during the 1930s and in 1980. The town's Sixth Form College is currently based in the former grammar school buildings.

Design work for the Victorian grammar school buildings was carried out by George Gordon Hoskins (1837-1911) who was based in Russell Street Buildings, Northgate from 1864. Much of his work during the late 1860s was commissioned by local Quaker families and included 'Westbrook' for Henry Pease in 1865, 'Elm Ridge' on Carmel Road South for John Pease in 1867 (which was converted into a Methodist Church in 1932) and 'Woodburn'—demolished in 1930—for John Pease's daughter, Sophia and her husband Theodore Fry.

Many of these buildings, including the grammar school premises, show the influence of Alfred Waterhouse for whom Hoskins had previously served as clerk of works. Hoskins' first book, *Designs for Chimney Pieces* 1871, was dedicated to Alfred Waterhouse and he wrote two further books: *Clerk of the Works: A Vade Mecum for all engaged in the Superintendence of Building Operation* (published in 1876) and *An Hour with the Sewer Rat:a few plain hints on house drainage and sewer gas* (1879).

George Gordon Hoskins also found time to serve in several areas of public life. He became a conservative councillor for Darlington East Ward in 1881 and for the West Ward nine years later. In 1892 he took office as J.P. for Darlington and filled the same post for County Durham in 1908. Hoskins' public spirited approach spread into other areas of town life and he was prominent in local church matters up to his death in 1911.

Darlington's growth as an industrial and commercial centre during the second half of the 19th century brought the need for improved medical facilities and in 1865 the town's first public hospital opened in Russell Street. It replaced an earlier Dispensary but, following the opening of Hundens Lane Isolation Hospital in 1874 and the Greenbank Hospital during 1885, the Russell Street building was taken over as the Conservative Club. The grey-brick New Hospital buildings in Greenbank Road were designed by George Gordon Hoskins and construction work took place between 1883-85. Additional construction work was later carried out, with design work by Hoskins, but during the inter-war years the town's main focus of medical care shifted to a site on Hollyhurst Road with the construction of the Memorial Hospital. It was officially opened on Friday, 5 May 1933 by His Royal Highness the Prince George, K.G., G.C.V.O. and recent expansion of facilities led to the closure of hospital facilities on Greenbank Road followed by the demolition of buildings during 1997.

Quaker families began to settle in Darlington in the 1660s and they soon became prominent in the town's economic development. Woollen and linen industries became increasingly centralised in their hands and during this period of late 18th-century prosperity the population increased from around 3,500 in 1767 to over 4,500 by 1801. Some residential development took place in the late 18th century at the top of Blackwellgate, Bondgate and Northgate. A considerable increase in population occurred during the second decade of the 19th century and between 1800 and 1850 the town's population increased to more than 12,000.

Much of this demographic activity resulted from the opening of the Stockton & Darlington Railway in September 1825. Inspired by one of the town's leading Quaker citizens, Edward Pease, the railway not only improved Darlington's trading links but also gave rise to several associated industries, including locomotive, carriage and wagon building and the production of raw materials such as iron and steel. Terraced housing for the growing workforce was soon crammed into adjacent building plots. Overall production of iron and steel also increased with the result that by 1867 there were three blast furnaces, 153 puddling furnaces and nine finishing mills in the town.

The locomotive works closed in 1966 after 103 years of engine building but there are reminders of railway history in the town's two station buildings. North Road Station was built in 1842 to replace an earlier station. Sash windows and a cast-iron colonnade give it the external appearance of a domestic dwelling but since 1975 the interior space has served as a railway museum. Pride of place is given to Stephenson's Locomotion No.1, which hauled the first train on the Stockton & Darlington Railway when it was opened on 27 September 1825. All around there are early engines and carriages as well as smaller items of memorabilia. Close by is the Skerne Railway Bridge. Dating from 1825, it was designed by the Durham County architect, Ignatius Bonomi, and probably represents the first railway bridge to be designed by an architect.

Bank Top Station on Victoria Road is a fine example of the work of William Bell, architect to the North Eastern Railway. His scheme was completed in 1887 and features a huge red brick clock tower at the Victoria Road entrance along with a superb cast iron roof over the railway tracks.

The statue of Joseph Pease (1799-1872) stands in a prominent position at the north end of High Row. Four bronze panels around the plinth illustrate important episodes in his career: politics, education, railways and the anti-slavery movement. The influence of Quaker families such as Pease and Backhouse is found in many parts of the town. On the north side of Houndgate—close to the market place—is 'Pease's House', birthplace of Edward Pease (1767-1858), father of Joseph and one of the promoters of the Stockton & Darlington Railway. Northgate Lodge, a bow-fronted house dating from 1830, was at one time the home of John Beaumont Pease (a nephew of Edward Pease) and the design work of Sir Alfred Waterhouse is evident in Mowden Hall—built in 1881 for Edward Lucas Pease—and Arthur Pease's residence at Hummersknott.

Waterhouse was also responsible for designing the group of buildings including the old town hall—dating from 1864—the market hall and the clock tower which was a gift to the town of Joseph Pease. Close by, towards the northern end of High Row, is Barclay's Bank, formerly Backhouse's Bank. It was designed by Sir Alfred Waterhouse in the Victorian Gothic style and was also completed in 1864.

Successive generations of the Pease family continued to play a part in the development of railways throughout the north east of England. Notable among these influential Quaker businessmen was Henry Pease (1807-1881), a grandson of Edward Pease. His early working years were spent in the leather-making business and an involvement with politics led to him becoming Darlington's first mayor and then M.P. for South Durham from 1857-1865. In the field of railway development he was the driving force behind the Middlesbrough and Guisborough line (opened in 1854), Darlington to Barnard Castle (opened on 8 July 1856) and the line between Barnard Castle and Tebay (opened on 4 July 1861). This 35-mile route crossed stretches of wild Pennine moorland and construction work lasted almost five years. Extensive engineering schemes were necessary—often in the form of huge bridges and viaducts that crossed deep valleys. (Most notable of these was the Belah Viaduct which measured 1040 ft. in length and had a maximum height of 196 ft.)

The extension of the Stockton & Darlington Railway from Redcar to Saltburn in August 1861 presented fewer engineering problems. Two years previously (in 1859) Henry Pease had formed the Saltburn Improvement Company which was charged with building an entirely new holiday resort on the impressive North Yorkshire cliff-top setting. This 'New Jerusalem' was to attract upper-class Victorian holidaymakers and, in keeping with its jewelled image, there was a great emphasis on stylish shops, ornate gardens and luxurious hotel accommodation. It was appropriate that Henry Pease should coordinate celebrations in Darlington during 1875 to mark the Golden Jubilee of the Stockton & Darlington Railway.

Several of the town's 19th-century buildings were designed by J.P. Pritchett. These include the Mechanics' Institute on Skinnergate which dates from 1853. Skinnergate also has several examples of the town's 'yards', which housed workers and their families. On the east side, between Skinnergate and High Row, are 'Mechanics' Yard', 'Clark's Yard' and 'Buckton's Yard', while on the opposite side is 'Friends' Yard'.

During the second half of the 19th century, the population of Darlington increased to over 45,000 and in 1867 a new borough was established. Along with the market hall and old town hall (dating from 1864), several other notable buildings were completed during this period. Edward Pease (1834-1880) provided money to build the library in Crown Street which opened in 1885 and was extended in 1933. Outside the red sandstone and pressed brick building is a small boulder with a metal ring. A former editor of the *Northern Echo*, W.T. Stead, often used it to tether his pony after travelling to his nearby office from the family home at Grainey Hill Cottage, Hummersknott. In 1880 Mr. Stead moved to London to become editor of the *Pall Mall Gazette* and was drowned in the Titanic disaster of 1912.

In Northgate is the original Technical College building which was opened by the Duke of Devonshire in 1897. A large glacial boulder, known as Bulmer's Stone, stands in front of the college building and takes its name either from the Bulmer family who owned adjacent property or from a town crier, Willie Bulmer, who is said to have stood on the stone to read news items to townsfolk.

Several Darlington menfolk have found a place in military history. Two of the four serving Bradford brothers were awarded the Victoria Cross during the First World War. Roland Boys Bradford was awarded the Military Cross at the age of 25 and was the youngest Brigadier General in the British army when he gained the Victoria Cross. He was killed in action at Cambrai in 1917 and his widow received the award two years later. His achievements are recorded by an inscription at St Cuthbert's Church, a plaque and memorial window in Holy Trinity Church on Woodlands Road and a porch at the town's Memorial Hospital.

Another of the Bradford brothers, R.N. Lieutenant Commander George Nicholson Bradford, was posthumously awarded the V.C. for his part in the raid on Zeebrugge during 1918.

Michael Murphy is one of only four V.C. holders to forfeit the medal for later misdeeds. During the Indian Mutiny of 1872 he was a comrade of another of the town's foremost military leaders, Sir Henry Havelock-Allan, and it was Murphy's actions at Nathupur which led to his award. This former Darlington ironworker was later found guilty of stealing a sack of oats and hay and, when the terms of a royal warrant of 1856 were enforced, his punishment was severe. He forfeited the Victoria Cross, lost a £10 annual pension and received a nine months' prison sentence (with hard labour). After spending his later years in poverty, Michael Murphy died in 1893 aged 63 and a headstone marks his grave in the town's North Cemetery.

The growing 19th-century township received water from pumps installed on premises beside the Tees at Broken Scar in 1849. After settlement, treatment and filtration, the water was delivered into Darlington, but, as demand for water increased, further treatment capacity was established on the north side of Coniscliffe Road. In 1926 a major expansion of installations was completed but original machinery was retained as a back-up.

Modernisation of the treatment plant brought an increase in capacity during 1955 and in 1972 another extension was added to the 13 million gallon per day plant. During 1980 original buildings at the Tees Cottage pumping station were threatened with demolition but in November of that year a charitable trust was formed to preserve buildings and equipment and since then members have carried out restoration work on both, including the three pumping systems (steam, gas and electric) which were the height of innovation in their time.

The origins of modern theatre can probably be traced back to medieval miracle plays that were performed at places such as York and Chester. During the Elizabethan period, groups of travelling players toured provincial towns but the wave of popularity that stemmed from the writings of William Shakespeare and his contemporaries was checked by the period of the Interregnum (1649-1660) under Oliver and Richard Cromwell. The restoration of the monarchy under Charles II brought a resurgence of interest in the theatre and although this prosperity continued during the 18th century the country's only purpose-built theatres were to be found in London.

In 1766 a former tithe barn at Stockton on Tees was converted into a theatre and nearby Richmond gained a theatre in 1788; it was probably the influence of Darlington's Quaker citizens that inhibited similar developments in the town. During the early 1800s, Thorn's Theatre was set up in Clay Row before moving to premises in Blackwellgate. Several other theatrical ventures were short-lived including the first Theatre Royal, in Buck's Close, which closed in 1865 and a new Theatre Royal which opened in Northgate in 1881 but was soon destroyed by fire. A third Theatre Royal opened in 1887 and continued in use until 1936.

Darlington's oldest surviving theatre, the Hippodrome, opened in Parkgate on 2 September 1907 under the management of Signor Rino Pepi, an Italian who gave up a stage career to concentrate on running theatrical venues in the north east. The early years brought an array of star performers including Harry Lauder, George Robey, Florrie Forde and Evelyn Laye. Rino Pepi died on 17 November 1927, hours before an appearance by the legendary ballerina, Pavlova, and by this time the theatre was suffering severe financial difficulties. A local syndicate of businessmen bought the building for £18,500 but the 1930s brought more financial crises and regular changes in management. In 1936 a flamboyant theatrical entrepreneur named Teddy Hinge took over at the Hippodrome and attracted audiences over the next 20 years with a mixture of titillating shows such as 'Bare Skins and Blushes' and 'Laughter and Lovelies' as well as new entertainers like Nellie Wallace, Frankie Vaughan and Tommy Cooper.

After a short period of closure the theatre was reopened by Darlington Amateur Operatic Society in 1958 and, following a major programme of cleaning and refurbishment, the Society's production of 'White Horse Inn' was a major success. Few more productions were staged over the next few years and although the building was purchased by Darlington Corporation for £8,000 in 1964 (with full control two years later) after which further improvements were made, the theatre's fortunes remained at a low ebb. The turning point came in 1972 when Peter Tod was appointed theatre director and within five years he had increased audiences from 20 per cent capacity to almost 85 per cent. A performance by Dame Margot Fonteyn in January 1976 was compared with the appearance of Pavlova in 1927 and, with entertainers of the calibre of Dorothy Tutin, Sir Michael Redgrave, Phyllis Calvert, Sacha Distel and Ken Dodd attracting large audiences, the theatre's 80th anniversary was marked with the news that average attendances of 95 per cent represented the highest audiences of any provincial theatre. A thriving 'Friends' group led an appeal to reseat the whole auditorium during 1982 and in 1990 the theatre was closed for 10 months while a £1.5 million scheme increased seating capacity from 600 to 900 and updated facilities throughout the building. These schemes have ensured that Darlington Civic Theatre retains its place as one of the country's foremost provincial theatres.

During the Edwardian period, housing development had almost reached the village of Cockerton and it was incorporated in 1915. On the eastern side of the town, Haughton-le-Skerne was added in 1930.

During periods of industrial expansion, Darlington maintained its place as the market town for a large agricultural hinterland and this is illustrated by successive schemes to remodel the market place. In 1894 the *Hat and Feathers* public house, along with adjacent cottages, was demolished to improve the view from the market place to St Cuthbert's Church and further schemes have culminated with repaving of the central area during the mid-1990s.

Several pleasant 18th-century buildings survive on the south side of the market place. Bennet House, a tall three-storey brick house on the corner of Bull Wynd, was reduced in size when the adjacent roadway was widened but is still one of the town's finest surviving Georgian buildings. Just beyond the south-eastern corner of the market place is the new town hall. Built on the site of the Bishop of Durham's manor house (which was demolished in 1970), it was designed by Williamson and Faulkner-Brown of Newcastle in conjunction with the Borough Architect and officially opened by H.R.H. Princess Anne on 27 May 1970.

Other town-centre schemes reflect Darlington's continued prosperity. A large sporting and leisure complex, the Dolphin Centre, has been developed on the southern side of the market place while the prestigious Cornmill Shopping Centre covers a large sector of ground between Tubwell Row, Northgate and Crown Street. Another chapter in the town's municipal history opened on 1 April 1997 when Darlington became a unitary authority and this busy south Durham township—with a proud past—seems assured of further rounds of future prosperity.

1 A busy scene on 5 August 1905 when Earl Roberts unveiled the South African War Memorial that stands close to Stone Bridge over the river Skerne. A guard of honour at the ceremony was provided by the 1st Volunteer Battalion of the Durham Light infantry. (As a military commander, General Frederick S. Roberts had distinguished himself in the Afghan and South African wars around the turn of this century.)

2 Geese are gathered at the entrance to St Cuthbert's churchyard. At one time the herding of animals, and in this case, birds, would have been a familiar sight as farmers drove their stock along the lanes and byways leading to Darlington and its frequent markets.

3 Darlington's official reception for local troops returning from the Boer War in 1901. Celebrations are centred around the old town hall and market place.

4 The town's development during medieval times owes much to its emergence as a market centre for the South Durham and North Yorkshire areas. The mock half-timbered wall of the *Boot and Shoe Hotel* on the north side forms a back cloth to this busy scene where an assortment of headwear is displayed by the assembled menfolk. (Another public house, the *Hat and Feather* Vaults, was attached to the *Boot and Shoe* until demolition took place at the end of the 19th century.)

5 This scene illustrates the importance of Darlington as a market centre. Even in these earlier days farmers and traders faced the problem of where to park the cart and hitch the horse. Note the advertisement for Mr. Sharp, Pawnbroker, high above the rooftops.

6 A Monday market in 1950. The old coffee stall is positioned in front of St Cuthbert's church gates and the power station's chimneys and cooling towers (demolished in 1978) dominate the sky line.

7 A general view of the Horse Market (and canopy which forms part of the covered market) in the 1930s showing a range of motor vehicles. The premises of W.H. Smith & Son are on the right and the impressive town hall is prominent on the left.

8 An aerial view of Darlington looking northwards in the early 1960s. The old town hall, covered market and market place occupy a central site with High Row, Bondgate and Northgate prominent as main routes through the town centre. On the right of the photograph is Pease's Mill—with its high chimney—on the banks of the Skerne. Originally a worsted mill, in later years it produced man-made fibres. At the top left corner are streets of 19th-century industrial terraced houses for railway workers.

9 A rooftop view of central Darlington showing High Row (on the left) and Northgate in the distance beyond the group of buildings comprising the Clock Tower and Market Hall. Designed by Alfred Waterhouse, the Clock Tower was a gift to the town by Joseph Pease and dates from 1864.

10 Horses and carriages at the northern end of High Row in the early 1900s, looking towards the town hall and the market hall in the distance. The terraced roadway on the right replaced a gentle slope in 1901 and the statue of Joseph Pease M.P. (1799-1872) has four bronze panels showing phases from his career: politics, education, railways and the anti-slavery campaign. Note the *Borough Hotel*, which was adjacent to the *King's Head*, and other premises including a wine and spirit merchants.

11 A view looking northwards along High Row in the early 1900s. Alfred Waterhouse designed the clock tower, market hall and old town hall. The postcard dates from 1906 and was sent to an address in Whitby with news that the writer was getting two shillings for helping to make sweets. (Note the hansom cab and electric trams alongside the buildings on the right. The tram track ended in the near distance on High Row.)

12 A view from the northern end of High Row looking into Northgate during the early years of this century. The large brick-built *King's Head Hotel* (on the right) opened in 1893 and replaced a 17th-century coaching inn. Northgate formed part of the Great North Road until Darlington was by-passed in the 1960s. By the 1950s, at busy periods, through-traffic on the Great North Road came to a standstill at this traffic bottleneck.

13 A view looking southwards along High Row with the Pease statue and entrance to Bondgate on the right. A horse-drawn carriage stands close to the Pease statue while tramlines form overhead patterns. It is not difficult to see how the statue became a traffic hazard when motor vehicles became popular. It was moved to a safer site in 1958.

14 A general view of the central and northern sections of High Row in 1920 with the town hall and market hall on the right. Northgate runs away from High Row in the extreme right-hand distance and Bondgate slopes gently away to the left-hand side.

15 View of the northern end of High Row in about 1880 with the old *King's Head Inn* on the right and *Sun Inn*, with distinctive roof-top symbol, in the centre of the photograph. The street lamp on the left—at the entrance to Bondgate—was erected to celebrate the coronation of William IV and the entrance to Northgate is clearly seen on the right.

16   A cattle market taking place on the western side of High Row.

17   Celebrations on High Row—possibly marking the armistice of 1918.

18   The Pease statue and *King's Head Hotel* are prominent at the northern end of High Row—looking into Northgate.

19 A view of the Midland Bank, *King's Head Hotel* and Monument Rooms, close to the junction of High Row, Bondgate and Northgate, photographed in 1930. The Monument Rooms later known as Monument Chambers housed several insurance and financial offices.

20 The new *King's Head Hotel* pictured soon after building work was completed in 1893. An earlier building—also called the *King's Head*—was a stopping point for mail coaches travelling on the Great North Road between London and Newcastle upon Tyne.

21 A view looking northwards along High Row in 1930. Stationary traffic includes a range of motor cars, a delivery van and carts.

22 This postcard dates from July 1910 and features the *Bull's Head Hotel* and Mason's Dining Rooms as well as the impressive St Cuthbert's Church around the perimeter of the market place.

23 A view of Prebend Row dating from about 1890 with the *King's Head* behind the line of hackney carriages and the statue of Joseph Pease at the entrance to Bondgate.

24 A busy scene in Tubwell Row with carts lining the roadside as a tram makes its way up the slope towards High Row. The Spire of St Cuthbert's Church is prominent in the right-hand distance and the projecting roof of the covered market is visible on the extreme right.

25 A view along Tubwell Row in 1907 looking eastwards down the slope towards the river Skerne. (This thoroughfare derives its name from a well that supplied household water.) The premises of Allison's (ironmongers) and Kent and Brydon (seed merchants) dominate the left side with Sharp's pawnbrokers on the right. The spire of St Cuthbert's Church dominates the skyline.

26 A view of Tubwell Row in 1920 looking eastwards towards Stone Bridge with the spire of St Cuthbert's in the distance. A fountain and lamp occupy a central position on the roadway.

27 Small-scale premises on the north side of Tubwell Row, photographed in 1959. The buildings on the right were demolished soon afterwards to make way for the North Eastern Co-operative Store. This in turn has been replaced by the Cornmill Shopping Complex.

28 The old *Nag's Head Inn* dominates this view of Tubwell Row in 1916. Demolition took place in 1963 and a new building was erected on the site. Tram lines for the town's electric trams are prominent in the roadway.

29 A view of Church Lane behind the *Nag's Head Inn*, photographed in 1916. Some of the 17th-century brickwork survives today. (The original building was a vicarage.)

30 The old Stone Bridge and Ropery Yard. To the left of the photograph is the junction of Tubwell Row and Crown Street—pictured in about 1894. The ropeworks was operated by a company that later moved to Bedale and was well-known for marquee hire, Clapham's of Bedale.

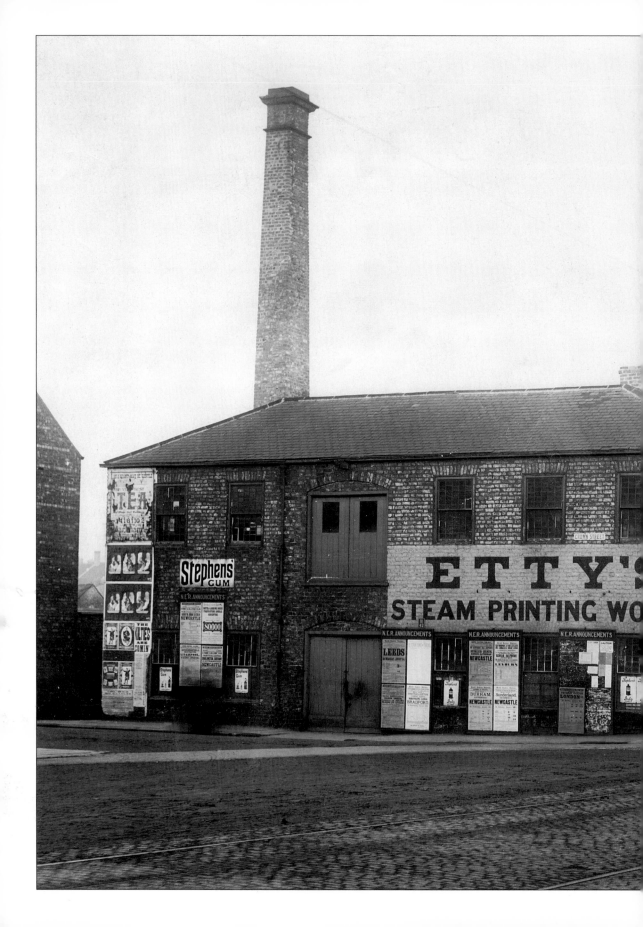

31 The approach to Stone Bridge at the junction of Tubwell Row and Crown Street, with the track and gantry for electric tramcars. The chimney behind Etty's steam printing works served a tannery beside the river Skerne.

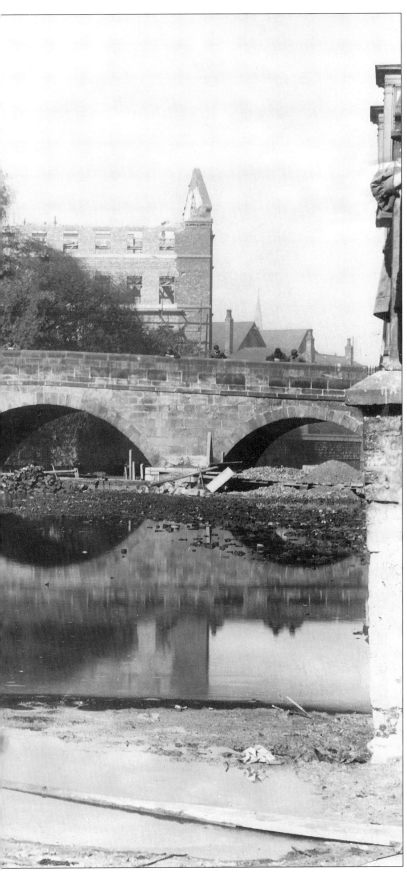

32 The old Stone Bridge across the Skerne after the fire at Pease's Mill in 1894. Wooden piles driven into the river bed beside the bridge are preparatory stages of work to replace this structure with a metal bridge that continues in use today. Ironically, it is still referred to as 'Stonebridge'.

33 A rooftop view of central Darlington dating from 1938. Towering over the clutter of gabled roofs is the chimney of Pease's Mill on a site overlooking the river Skerne.

34 A rooftop view over Darlington in 1940 with power station buildings (constructed between 1937 and 1939) dominating the horizon. St Cuthbert's Church covers land in the foreground and the *Boot and Shoe Hotel*, with mock timbered gable, marks the northern edge of the market place.

35 An ink and water-colour illustration entitled 'In Bondgate—on a slide' from the album, *Family Annals by road and rail by road and field* published in 1840 by Samuel Tuke Richardson of Darlington and Piercebridge.

36 Bulmer's Stone photographed in 1890 outside cottages on Northgate, Darlington. The large square-shaped stone is a glacial erratic and is known to have originated on Shap Fell, Cumbria. It is probably named after William Bulmer, the town crier, who stood on it to read the news (or after the Bulmer family who owned property in Northgate). The stone may also have been used for beating yarn when Darlington had a flourishing linen industry. The adjacent weavers' cottages were demolished in 1897 to make way for the town's Technical College but the stone remains near its original site.

37 Bondgate pictured in about 1890. The old *King's Head Hotel* is prominent in the distance with Pease's chimney immediately behind. Skinnergate is on the right. The old manor of Bondgate was separate from the adjacent Borough of Darlington with inhabitants holding land by bond-tenure rather than as freeholders (in the Borough). This quiet scene was transformed with the arrival of the horsefair which filled a large section of the thoroughfare.

38   A busy day at the horse fair in Bondgate during 1890. (Darlington was an important centre for horse sales as well as market produce.) Tram lines run down the central section of the highway but most people are making use of an older means of transport in the form of horse and cart.

39   A general view of Bondgate in 1930. The motor cycle and sidecar on the left and the central tram posts are reminders of contemporary forms of transport.

40 The junction of Bull Wynd and Houndgate with the gable of central hall on the left of the photograph. Houndgate derives its name from the days when hounds were taken along this route to join hunts in the forest of Blackwell on the south-west side of the town. Bull Wynd takes its name from its close proximity to the site of bull baiting activities (in front of the old town hall) and the *Bull Inn*. Inset stones on the west side of the Wynd serve as reminders of the *Bull Inn* and the Bulmer family.

41 A view along Bondgate showing the Fothergill Temperance Fountain which was moved to South Park. The fountain was erected by public subscription in memory of Dr. John Fothergill, president of Darlington Total Abstinence Society (1835-1858), in 1862 and moved to a site in South Park 12 years later.

42 Horse-drawn vehicles line the sides of Blackwellgate at its junction with Houndgate.

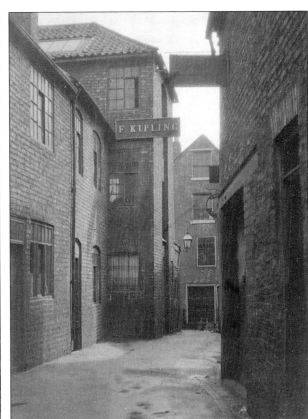

43 Two horse-drawn trams occupy central positions in High Northgate.

44 Mechanics Yard, photographed in the mid-1920s.

45 A postcard dated 1907 shows the view along Blackwellgate. Skinnergate is on the left, with Houndgate sloping away on the right.

46 The workforce, of North Road Locomotive Works leaves for their midday break on this postcard dated 1908.

47 A quiet scene on Northgate in 1910 with the spire of St George's Church in the distance. Much of this view is now sited outside the modern ring road.

48 A view of Northgate in 1910 from outside the General Post Office which was situated on the right. The *Three Tuns Inn* to the left was one of numerous town centre hostelries. Although this inn no longer exists the town still contains a large number of watering holes!

49 Looking northwards along North Road with several single-decker trolley buses on the right-hand side of the thoroughfare awaiting workers from North Road Locomotive Works.

50 A general view of Northgate in 1930. Trolley buses are prominent on both sides of the roadway but bicycles appear to be the most popular form of transport. The building on the left of the trolley bus is the Prudential Insurance Office. Above the doorway is a statue of Prudence. This statue has been preserved by Darlington Council. In the centre is one of Darlington's electric trolley buses which ran—pollution free—until the 1950s.

51 A view of Skinnergate in 1948. The Court Cinema—which was later destroyed by fire—is prominent on the left, with the Mechanics Institute directly opposite. During the 19th century, Darlington had more than a hundred 'yards' and several examples of these are found in Skinnergate. On the west side are 'Friends School Yard', 'British School Yard', 'Punch Bowl Yard' and 'Burn's Yard'. On the east side—connecting Skinnergate with High Row—are 'Mechanics Yard', 'Clark's Yard' and 'Buckton's Yard'.

52 A view looking eastwards along Victoria Road in 1929. Bedford Street is on the right and the red-brick clock tower of Bank Top Station dominates the distant skyline. The station buildings date from 1887 and were the work of William Bell, architect to the North Eastern Railway.

53 The old railway 'cut' at the eastern end of Parkgate—close to Bank Top railway station pictured in about 1900. The 'cut' was widened in 1934-35 by removing the wall on the north side (left of the photograph). St John's Church is prominent in the distance and a public coal depot is sited on the north side of the cutting.

54 Looking eastwards along Victoria Road from a point near the junction with Grange Road. Feethams is behind the trees on the right and the tower of Bank Top Station is prominent in the distance. The large residential properties on the right were occupied by many of the town's professional people—dentists, clergymen, businessmen and a surgeon.

55 A view of Victoria Road—with the postmark 1906—looking towards the imposing tower and entrance to Bank Top Station. This part of Victoria Road supported a number of businesses which relied heavily on the close proximity of the station. These included three temperance hotels, many apartments and other small businesses.

56 A view of Victoria Road in 1920 looking eastwards. Bank Top Station covers high ground at the top of the slope and the Methodist New Connexion Church and *Speedwell Temperance Hotel* are prominent on the left. In recent years, the church has been used as a bathroom and tile showroom.

57 The entrance gates to Darlington Park feature on this postcard of 1906. It was posted in Darlington with a message arranging to meet a relative from Whitby at the station.

58 North Lodge Park was developed by Darlington Corporation in the grounds of North Lodge, former home of the Pease family. It opened in the early 1900s and this postcard, dated 9 September 1905, was sent to an address in Church Street, Whitby with the message 'arrived safe home and found all right ... Hoping you behaved well on your voyage'.

59 Views of the bandstand, lake and mock castle building (which served as a boathouse) in North Lodge Park. (The lake was drained in the 1930s and the castle feature was demolished during the 1960s.) This card was sent to his wife in Waterloo, near Liverpool, during April 1914 and the writer describes a tedious rail journey to Darlington via Leeds and Thirsk before explaining that he was about to have a game of bowls in the park.

60 The bandstand in North Lodge Park. The bandstand is a prominent feature within North Lodge Park which opened in 1903. It had a narrow escape in 1961 when the local police chief, Superintendent Arthur Mcguire, put forward plans for demolition of the bandstand and construction of a carpark for 300 vehicles.

61 A view of the River Skerne as it flows through South Park is featured on this post card dated 1905.

62 The Park House in South Park.

63 A monument to John Fowler in South Park, Darlington. Fowler, who married into the Pease family, invented a double acting steam drawn multi-furrow plough. The model was destroyed by vandals in the 1970s but the plinth is still in place in the South Park.

64 A view of the entrance to Southend Avenue (off Grange Road). Originally it was part of the Southend estate (developed by Pease) and the *Grange Hotel* was the large house, 'Southend'. The strip of woodland beside Southend Avenue is renowned for its display of crocuses during spring time.

65 An ornate fountain set into a roadside stone wall, with the date '1868'. It is one of eight cast-iron drinking fountains presented to the town by Joseph Pease. The best-preserved example of these fountains is to be found at the Milbank-Woodland Road junction.

66 Cast-iron drinking fountain with stone surround. This example is sited at the end of Milbank Road and another impressive fountain can be seen in the wall of the former *Grange Hotel* in Coniscliffe Road.

67 This bus shelter with decorative cast-iron supports stood on Haughton Road opposite the junction with Barton Street.

68 Darlington has much to offer those with an interest in architecture. Many buildings in the town bear fine decorative details and unusual combinations of stonework, brick and terracotta. Here is a magnificently bold example of a Victorian wrought-iron gate seen in Cleveland Terrace.

69 Pierremont became the home of the Quaker, Henry Pease, when he purchased the property in 1845 for £5,000. Ironically, it had been built in the 1830s by a non-Quaker, with the intention of out-doing existing Quaker mansions through its ornate Gothic style. Henry Pease took great pride in landscaping Pierremont's grounds and it became known as the 'Buckingham Palace of Darlington'.

70 Mowden Hall was built in 1881 for Edwin Lucas Pease, son of John-Beaumont Pease. It remained in the Pease family until 1927 after which it was used as a school, army headquarters and as an egg packing station! It is now occupied by the Department of Education and Science for dealing with teachers' pensions. It is uncertain whether the building is the work of Alfred Waterhouse or Norman Shaw.

71 'Woodlands' is situated on Woodlands Road opposite the end of Hollyhurst Road. Built by Robert Botcherby, a local timber merchant, it was later bought by Joseph Whitwell Pease, eldest son of Joseph Pease of Southend, Darlington. In recent years it was occupied by the late Sir William Lee, High Sheriff of County Durham, and then became office accommodation for a building firm. The extensive gardens have been partially developed with executive housing but, at the time of writing, the house is again unoccupied.

72 A general view of Darlington Free Library in 1910. Constructed of red sandstone and pressed brick, it was opened in 1885 and extended in 1933. (An art gallery and lecture room were created in the building and a local studies room was opened in 1970.)

73 A view along lower Priestgate in the 1960s showing the decorative terracotta and brickwork of the Edward Pease Public Library, the Pease's Mill chimney (built in 1872 and demolished in 1984) and the gable end of the Magnet Bowl—venue for a fashionable pastime during that decade.

74 Few north-east towns can boast such a fine Mechanics' Institute as this classical building by Pritchett. (Unusually this example has the lettering 'Mechanics' Institution' rather than Mechanics' Institute.) It was erected in 1853 and outside there is a good example of a Victorian cast-iron lamp standard from the days of the old County Borough of Darlington.

75 Grange Road Baptist Chapel was erected in 1873. This photograph dates from about 1908 and shows the original north-end entrance to the Avenue.

76 Bondgate Methodist Church in Saltyard was the work of Rev. William Jenkins, probably the most eminent designer of early 19th-century Methodist chapels.

77   The Liberal and Unionist Club and Offices at the junction of Gladstone Street and Northgate. Tram lines in the roadway run past the Darlington Technical College erected in 1897, in this photograph which dates from about 1910. It is easy to see why the club building was known as 'Ivy House'.

78 A Free Grammar School of Queen Elizabeth was founded by charter granted in 1563. The old school was closely dependent on the clergy of St Cuthbert's Church and was situated in Lead Yard until 1878 when this new school, designed by G.G. ('Pitch Pine') Hoskins was opened. In 1970 the grammar school became the Darlington Queen Elizabeth Sixth Form College.

79 & 80 The teacher training college was established in 1875 under the grand title of 'The British and Foreign Schools Society College for the Training of Mistresses for Elementary Schools. Designed by Pritchett, the college operated until the 1970s and in 1979 it was leased by Darlington Borough Council and reopened as the Arts Centre.

81 Part of Henry Pease's mid-19th-century development of the Pierremont estate included construction of a fishpond, ornamental gardens, an ice house and this gateway and clock tower which led to the naming of Tower Road.

82 Opened as the New Hippodrome and Palace of Varieties in 1907, the Darlington Civic Theatre is a superb example of an Edwardian music hall. Refurbished in recent years, with a canopy to match the original (seen in this photograph), the theatre is now extremely popular. The cast-iron tram pole and lamp standard has now gone.

83 Darlington Operatic Society still performs regularly at the town's Civic Theatre. Here we see Miss Joyce Banks (left) and an unknown member taking part in 'Our Miss Gibbs' in about 1935.

84 Staff pose for the camera in front of Robert Brown's provision stores at Harrowgate Hill on the town's northern perimeter. The post-war years saw the demise of many of these small businesses in the face of competition from large central retail outlets.

85 Staff of Gallon's Ltd., provision merchants, in front of the shop at Parkgate, Darlington in 1922. It is interesting to note that meat is displayed outside—an indication of lower levels of pollution and less stringent food health regulations— and that Danish butter is for sale at 2s. (10p) per pound.

86 A group of musicians in a Darlington yard at the turn of the century with an assortment of instruments including harmonium, several violins, piccolo and concertina. Possibly a family group making their own entertainment before the advent of radio and television.

87 Committee members and officials of Darlington (Eastbourne) Allotments, Limited. *Back Row*: H. Kendrew, F. Harrington, J.J. Young, J.M. Jones, A. Lascelles (J.P.), J. Wilcock (Vice Chairman), P. Timms, C. Stott. *Sitting*: A. Trees (Trustee), W. Grainger (Treasurer), E. Brennan (Chairman), R.M. Wrightson (Secretary), J.R. Rocket (Trustee). *Front Row*: T. Richmond, J. Kirby, J. Clark, T.A. Merrells. The name Lascelles is perpetuated in the naming of the 1960s estate at Eastbourne—Lascelles Park.

88 Group photograph of North Eastern Railway paint shop staff in 1910. The railway locomotive works was divided into a number of 'shops', each one specialising in a different process, for example, boiler shop, coppersmith's shop, blacksmith's shop, machine shop and paint shop. Each shop had its own bowler-hatted foreman.

89 Officials of the Darlington and Teesdale Naturalist Field Club at a tree planting ceremony in South Park, Darlington to celebrate Peace Day, 20 July 1919. Second from right is the park keeper, Mr. Morrison. Founded in 1891, the club is still very progressive and has included many prominent Quakers such as the Pease families, Mr. Edward Wooler and Dr. R.T. Manson, whose memorial (a large Snap granite boulder) stands within the entrance to South Park at Victoria Embankment.

90 A public Ambulance Service for Darlington was formed by subscription, at a total cost of £130, and the first horse ambulance began operations in 1905. The service was based in the old fire station in Borough Road and shared horses with the fire brigade. Many years later the ambulance body was placed on a Ford motor chassis and continued in service for several more years.

91 A detachment of Whessoe Ltd.'s Home Guard photographed during the Second World War. Until the closure of Whessoe Engineering works in recent years, the company was a major employer in the town and during the post-Second World War years it was well known for the manufacture of pressure vessels, steel storage tanks, chemical plant equipment and gas cleaning plant. Most local heavy industries had their own home guard detachment during the Second World War.

92 Dr. Algernon Fothergill (1868-1945) was born at Leamington, studied medicine at Edinburgh University and established a medical practice in Darlington. In his spare time he was greatly involved in local field sports such as hunting, riding and shooting. He used his skill as a draughtsman to illustrate many books on field sports and gave up medicine to become a full-time artist. This drawing combines his love of hunting with the local political scene.

93 & 94 R.T. Snaith, builder, carpenter, joiner and undertaker, did a great deal of quality work in churches and secular buildings throughout the area. This tradition continued when the firm was taken over by R. Blackett & Son. Here we see two shopfitting jobs. Firstly the exterior of Moyler's sweet shop at 13a, Bondgate, and secondly, Hinton's grocer's shop in Bondgate. Both date from the 1939-45 period.

95 One of Darlington's legendary figures was 'Geordie' Fawbert. Born in 1874, he became a likeable rogue and was not renowned for his appearance. He dabbled in various business ventures including selling mussels and fish, coal, building work, running a bus service and cycle shop. Here he is the hatless young man seen outside his shop on Clay Row.

96 Darlington Quoits Club was established in 1846 and still exists today. The annual competition was for the Silver Quoit and was played for on a pitch at the rear of the Central Hall (now part of the Dolphin Centre). Numbered among these members in 1860 are many local businessmen. Thomas Potts, seated left, was a tobacco manufacturer in partnership with Mr. Swinburne (centre standing). The man seated far right is Richard Graham, a gardener at Pierremont or Brinkburn.

97 St Paul's, Darlington, football team photographed during the 1903-4 season. That season they played 23 matches of which they won 11, lost 7, drew 5—gaining 27 points.

98 Detail from a bill head of Thomas Morritt, publican of the *Three Tuns* and *Post Office Hotel,* Darlington, dated *c.*1860. *The Three Tuns* was in Northgate, almost directly opposite the old General Post Office. By 1900 it was simply *The Three Tuns* under a landlady, Mrs. Ann Turnbull.

99 The 1930s' art deco-style frontage of S. Tetley & Sons Ltd., tobacconists and confectioners, based in Skinnergate, Darlington. It is an example of the shop fitting work of R.T. Snaith & Sons of Darlington who were later taken over by the well-known Darlington firm of Blacketts.

100 A once-familiar sight on the streets of Darlington was the Co-operative Society milkman. This photograph shows a proud milkman (or drayman) holding a silver cup awarded to the splendidly turned out horse and float in a show.

101 During the 1950s the horse was replaced by the electric milk float. The new vehicle is seen outside the Model Dairy in Melland Street, off Borough Road, Darlington.

102 The size of the Darlington Co-operative Society's Bakery Department delivery van (as seen in 1946) illustrates the extent of the Co-operative Society's business in the town.

103 The Darlington Co-operative and Industrial Society's central stores and offices was In Priestgate. In 1900 the premises included grocers, butchers, milliners, tailors, dressmakers and boot dealers. In the 1960s a modern extension was added to the Tubwell Row elevation. This was built around the *Raby Hotel* whose brewery owners would not sell. The whole area was cleared in preparation for the construction of the Cornmill Shopping Centre which opened in 1992.

104 The Distinctive brick and glass frontage of the Co-operative Society's self-service store in Darlington. In common with many north-eastern industrial areas the Darlington Co-operative shops and later stores were well patronised by the large numbers of manual workers and their families. Many people will still be able to recall their Co-op dividend number.

105 A Darlington co-operative advertisement takes central position among a variety of posters on bill boards alongside a local street in 1948. Until the 1950s a number of large hoardings dominated positions on many main roads but modern planning controls have restricted this form of display.

106 Fox's oriental café and creamery was sited close to the *King's Head Hotel* in Northgate and the company Fox and Sons were also tea dealers and coffee roasters. The photograph dates from 1910.

107 Darlington Forge was renowned for making many massive steel and iron forgings and castings for the shipbuilding industry. These included rudders, stern frames and crankshafts for such well-known ships as HMS *Prince of Wales, King George V, Oceanic, Olympic* and *Britannic.*

108 This massive forge hammer, known as 'Tiny Tim', was used in the Albert Hill works of Darlington Forge Ltd. Here it is seen after demolition of the adjacent works buildings and it was later transported to the North of England Open Air Museum, Beamish, where it now features at the main entrance.

109   Darlington Forge Company Band. Darlington Forge began production in 1853 as little more than a blacksmith's shop but by the 1890s the firm's premises covered 30 acres and employed 800 men. In addition to castings for railways, the company manufactured the stern frames, rudder and propeller shaft brackets (weighing a total of 600 tons) for the *Queen Mary* and *Mauretania* as well as many other well-known vessels.

110   Splendid woodwork between the chancel arch at Barningham Church completed by J.T. Snaith of Darlington. The business was based in premises at 63-66 Bondgate until it was absorbed into Blackett's the builders. The Bondgate building has become licensed premises which still retain the name 'Blackett's'.

11 A steel roadway bridge under construction at the Cleveland Bridge and Engineering Company's yard at Darlington. The bridge was to span the Rio Cachoeirhina at Manaos in Brazil. It represents one example of the many bridges built for countries world-wide by this company. In 1981 they constructed what was then the world's longest suspension bridge, the Humber Bridge, and made the gates for the Thames Flood Barrier.

112 An area of the bridge yard at the Cleveland Bridge and Engineering Company's works at Darlington, showing Bessemer converters, blast furnace tubing and bridgework for the Southern Mahratta railway in India. These yards were in an area adjacent to Smithfield Road and the east coast main railway line until 1981 when they opened a new works at the Yarm Road site.

113 Another illustration entitled 'Love's Young Dream' from the publication covering the Sunday School Teachers' Conference at Darlington during August 1874.

114 A range of activities was held to mark the coronation of King Edward VII in 1902. In addition to a grand parade of schoolchildren, a huge bonfire and celebratory banquet, an ox was roasted in the town's market place. Slices of roast beef were sold on a commemorative plate featuring a picture of the roasting ox and listing members of the ox roasting committee as well as the mayor.

115 A party in Beaumont Street, Darlington on 19 July 1919. Several generations took part in celebrations at this time to mark the signing of a peace agreement after the First World War. It is worth noting the absence of men in the photograph and wondering how many of the families had lost a loved one in the war.

116 Black faced sheep face the camera at Darlington's annual show in 1920. A well-known farmer and stock breeder, Joseph William Dent, is on the right of the photograph.

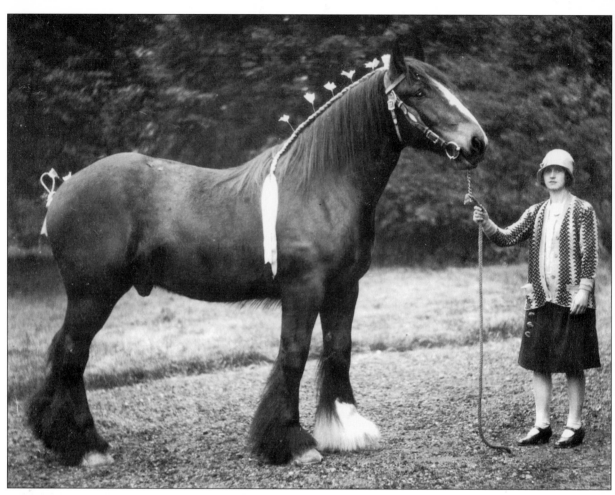

117 A locally-bred two-year-old shire horse, 'Rand Footprint' (Sire 'Pendley Footprint', Dam 'Bonnie Fashion') photographed in 1928. The horse won first prize as a three-year-old at the London Shire Horse Show in 1929 and first prize at the Great Yorkshire Show. The bridle is held by Ivy Metcalfe (née Sherwin).

118 Floral designs feature prominently in this group at the 'Grand Parade' during the celebration of Co-operation Day in early July 1930.

119 Horseman, Sid Richmond, is pictured holding the tether of a delivery horse at the 'Grand Parade' during Co-operation Day in July 1930.

120 On 24 October 1905, Princess Beatrice (Princess Henry of Battenberg—Queen Victoria's youngest daughter) and her daughter, Princess Ena (properly Princess Eugenie) opened a bazaar in the town in aid of the Greenbank Hospital. Princess Ena later became Queen Ena of Spain. Here we see the royal car with the 'royals' seated in the car.

121 A railway carnival float from the 1930s. The town's close links with the Stockton—Darlington Railway often featured in displays and 'Experiment' began service on the route on 10 October 1825. Among the flags and Christmas-style decorations, a touch of authenticity is added by the red flag which preceded locomotives on the actual line to give a warning to pedestrians.

122 A carnival float from the 1930s—with a humorous interpretation of an experimental locomotive (No.10,000) built at North Road Works in great secrecy. Owing to the confidential nature of the project, the locomotive became known as 'Hush Hush'. L.N.E.R. 10,000 was fitted with a water-tube boiler and ran over a million miles in service. The boiler was later used as a heater at Faverdale Works. Note the mistake in 'Mystery'.

123 Barmpton Hall at the tiny hamlet of Barmpton on the north-east side of Darlington. During the late 1700s Barmpton and nearby Ketton Halls were the residences of the Colling brothers, pioneering stock breeders of Durham short-horn cattle. In about 1880 workmen were building a new bridge over the river Skerne near to Barmpton when they unearthed an Iron-Age sword which was later sold to the British Museum for £25.

124 Ketton Hall was the home of Charles Colling, a well-known stock breeder. In 1784 he is said to have paid eight guineas for a bull from a neighbouring farmer and, after naming it 'Hubback', he used it to breed Durham shorthorns. He received the first ever 100-guinea fee paid for a shorthorn and, when he gave up farming, his bull, 'Comet' fetched 1,000 guineas.

125 The Colling Shorthorn Memorial Challenge Cup, presented by the Durham County Agricultural Committee to the Royal Agricultural Society of England in 1923. It was designed by Harrison & Sons, 'The County Goldsmiths Limited', Darlington.

126 Cockerton Bridge on Darlington's western outskirts, which carried the 'Coal Road' over the Cocker Beck to collieries in the West Auckland area. It was demolished in 1903 and its replacement was later widened to carry a tram system to Cockerton. The village of Cockerton has become a suburb of Darlington but the area around the Green retains its village atmosphere.

127 A view of the former *Punch Bowl Inn* as seen in 1900. It was converted to a farmhouse in the 1930s and is now a private residence.

128 The former *Punch Bowl Inn* at Blackwell pictured in 1987. Carmel Road South (on the right) has become one of the town's busiest suburban routes and the view is from the present post office looking towards Elm Ridge.

129 Blackwell cross roads viewed in the early 19th century, looking from north to south.

130 Blackwell cross roads looking from south to north in the early 20th century. The post office is on the left.

131 A four-seater Brougham carriage which operated during the period 1825-1850. It was purchased from Newbus Grange, Neasham near Darlington.

132 Darlington's place in railway history stems from the initiative and capital reserves of Edward Pease together with the engineering skills of George Stephenson. The result of their concerted efforts was the opening of the world's first steam hauled public passenger railway on 27 September 1825. The original engine, 'Locomotion', is now housed in Darlington Railway Centre and Museum after being on display outside North Road Station until 1890—where it is seen in this photograph—and then at Bank Top Station.

133 A Time Bill issued in 1825 giving details of the SDR Company's coach 'Experiment', during the railway's early operations in autumn 1825. The early passenger services operated by the SDR were by horse-drawn coaches and the journey time from Stockton to Darlington was two hours.

Stockton and Darlington Railway.

The COMPANY'S COACH

CALLED THE

EXPERIMENT,

Which commenced Travelling on MONDAY, the 10th of OCTOBER, 1825, will continue to run from *Darlington* to *Stockton*, and from *Stockton* to *Darlington* every Day, [Sunday's excepted] setting off from the DEPOT at each place, at the times specified as under, (viz.)

ON MONDAY,

From Stockton at half-past 7 in the morning, and will reach Darlington about half-past 9 ; the Coach will set off from the latter place on its return at 3 in the afternoon, and reach Stockton about 5.

TUESDAY,

From Stockton at 3 in the Afternoon, and will reach Darlington about 5.

On the following Days, viz. :—

WEDNESDAY, THURSDAY & FRIDAY,

From Darlington at half-past 7 in the Morning, and will reach Stockton about half-past 9 ; the Coach will set off from the latter place on its return at 3 in the Afternoon, and reach Darlington about 5.

SATURDAY,

From Darlington at 1 in the Afternoon, and will reach Stockton about 3.

Passengers to pay 1s. each, and will be allowed a Package of not exceeding 14 lb., all above that weight to pay at the rate of 2d. per Stone extra. Carriage of small Parcels 3d. each. The Company will not be accountable for Parcels of above £5 Value, unless paid for as such.

MR. RICHARD PICKERSGILL at his Office in Commercial Street, Darlington ; and MR. TULLY at Stockton, will for the present receive any Parcels and Book Passengers.

COPY OF TIME BILL ISSUED 1825.

134 An example of the early horse-drawn passenger coach services. This advertisement for the Stockton and Darlington Railway has details of fares and times.

135 Details of fares and times for steam-hauled passenger trains on the Stockton and Darlington Railway in 1840. Separate details of the market coach—on Mondays—illustrate the importance of Darlington's weekly market day.

136 Locomotion No.1 with the tender and coal waggons (with passengers on top) at the opening day of the Stockton and Darlington Railway. The illustration features in the book, *Sketches of Information as to Railroads* by Rev. James Adamson, Cupar, Fife, also an account of the *Stockton and Darlington Railway with Observations,* 1826.

137 The railway cavalcade is shown crossing the Skerne bridge at Darlington preceded by a man on a horse with red flag. This romanticised view of Darlington situated on a hilltop employs an amount of artistic licence.

138 Original Stockton—Darlington station buildings at Fighting Cocks. The station master's house is on the right and in the distance is the circular tower of the local windmill and the tapering chimney of Middleton St George Ironworks.

139 North Road Station stands on the original 1825 Stockton and Darlington Railway and part of this building was constructed in 1842 by the company and later extended by the North Eastern Railway. For many years this station served both east- and west-bound routes whilst Bank Top station served north-south trains. North Road Station now houses the Darlington Railway Centre and Museum.

140 An illustration of the Railway Workmen's Institute situated on the corner of North Road and Whessoe Road close to the North Road Locomotive Works where the majority of its members were employed. It appeared in *The British Workman* for September 1863 which is the same year that the N.E.R. works opened.

141 & 142 The North Eastern Railway Locomotive Works were opened in 1863 and for the next century the premises employed more workers than any other company in the town. The works was divided into a series of 'shops' (workshops) each of which specialised in an aspect of locomotive construction, for example, boiler shop, blacksmiths, wheel shop etc.

143 On 15 November 1910 a Newcastle—Leeds freight train careered into a second goods train travelling from Newcastle to Hull (as the Hull-bound train was stationary on the fast line outside Bank Top station, Darlington). The driver and fireman of the second train were both killed and the cause of the accident was never determined.

144 North Road railway bridge looking north away from the town centre. The bridge carries a section of the Stockton & Darlington Railway and the original S. & D.R. booking office was situated at the far side of the bridge. The famous Skerne Bridge—seen on the £5 note—is a few yards to the right and North Road Station is to the left.

145 Wrecked carriages and track side signals after the crash on 27 June 1928 just outside the Bank Top Station. Two trains collided. One was an excursion train from Newcastle Upon Tyne to Scarborough and the other was an express goods train bound for London. Twenty-five people were killed and 45 were injured. Two of the coaches on the excursion train had telescoped and the engine of the goods train was completly de-railed.

146 Steam locomotive No.62768 ex LNER 4-4-0 Class D49 at Darlington Works photographed on 26 October 1952.

147 Opening of the Darlington tramway system, known as Darlington Corporation Light Railway. The ceremony was performed on 1 June 1904. Large crowds have gathered on Prebend Row (at the north end of High Row) to watch the procession of tram cars after the opening ceremony.

148 Two tram cars from Darlington Light Railway. The mayoress, Mrs. A. Henderson, and Mrs. J.J. Wilkes performed the opening ceremony before posing for photographs at the controls of the tramcars.

DARLINGTON LIGHT RAILWAYS, OPENED 1st JUNE, 1904.

Car Driven by the Mayoress (Mrs. Henderson).

Car Driven by Mrs. Wilkes.

149   European entertainers often visited this country and this group of itinerant Italian musicians are pictured outside the door of Dinsdale rectory in March 1892. Their instruments resemble traditional Northumbrian pipes.

150 Children pictured on their way to the village school at Low Dinsdale in 1910, with the tower of St John the Baptist Church in the distance. The children with bags are probably carrying their lunches as a school meals service was not compulsory until 1944 (under the terms of the 'Butler' Education Act).

151 Fishlocks Mill on the river Tees at Low Dinsdale. The man-made barrier caused lengthy controversy and was finally removed in the early 1900s although adjacent properties—close to the village of Dinsdale—retain the name 'Fishlocks'.

152 Dinsdale Weir and Fishlocks Mill, photographed in about 1890.

153 A trio of ladies on the downstream side of Dinsdale Weir and Fishlocks in the 1890s.

154 & 155 Views of the ruined chapel at Sockburn. Much of the stonework dates from the 13th century but earlier buildings saw the consecration of Higbald of Lindisfarne in A.D. 780 and Eanbald as Archbishop of York in A.D. 796. The Conyers Chapel, on the north side of the ruins, was restored in the early 1900s in order to house relics from the church.

156 The restored Conyers Chapel houses a number of pre-Conquest relics including hogbacks, sections of stone crosses and medieval effigies. One of the effigies has been cited as that of Sir John Conyers who is credited with putting an end to the Sockburn Worm that had terrorised the district.

The style of the effigy dates from before his time, but the Conyers family certainly gained land in the Sockburn area. Other reminders of the legend are found in the broadsword—supposedly used to slay the monster—and a ceremony on nearby Croft Bridge when the sword is handed to an incoming Bishop of Durham.

157 Members of the Cardwell family skating on the frozen river Tees at Low Coniscliffe in the severe winter of January 1940. In the background is the old Merrybent railway bridge which carried the mineral railway from Barton Quarry to Darlington. It was demolished in 1965 and a road bridge now carries the A1(M) over the river at this point.

158 A view of the eastern side of Piercebridge village green in 1905 showing St Mary's Church (dating from 1873) and adjacent cottages. The modern settlement at Piercebridge is built within the perimeter of a Roman fort—built in about A.D. 300—enclosing ten and a half acres of land. Recent excavations of the Roman site uncovered a range of buildings along the eastern side of the village. The remains have been consolidated and are open to the public with access from a lane alongside St Mary's Church.

159 High Coniscliffe village in about 1900. The three prominent buildings on the left beyond the quarries are St Edwin's Church, the school and rectory. One of the area's first golf courses was developed along the nearby riverbanks and properties beside the main road include the original clubhouse.

160 Cockerton village on Darlington's north-west perimeter. The green is triangular in shape with mainly 18th-century properties around the edge. By the early 1900s housing had spread from central Darlington almost as far as Cockerton and it was incorporated in 1915.

161 Aycliffe lies five miles to the north of Darlington beside the river Skerne and is cut through by the old Great North Road (A167). The tranquility of the village green contrasts sharply with the bustle of the 'new town' at nearby Newton Aycliffe.

162 The old *Scotch Corner Inn* photographed in 1934. The lady standing with the tandem is Marjorie Clark. During the early summer of 1939, the inn was demolished and replaced by a larger red-brick building.

163 An absence of traffic allows pedestrians to stand in the roadway at Fighting Cocks in the parish of Middleton St George. The *Fighting Cocks Inn* became a stopping point for traffic on the Stockton-Darlington railway until station buildings were completed close by.

164 A stone bridge was built across the river Tees at Croft in about 1400 on the orders of Bishop Skirlaw. Its seven ribbed and pointed arches were restored in 1673 and the road surface is now twice its original width. Down the years it has been the setting for an interesting and unusual ceremony where newly-appointed Bishops of Durham have been presented with the Conyers falchion by a representative of the Lord of Sockburn. (See photographs of Sockburn, nos. 154-6.)

165 Until the construction of modern road systems, the A167 road was a vital north-south link and until 1879 the bridge had a toll gate at the northern end (left of the photograph). The *Croft Spa Hotel* can be seen across the bridge. Situated just downstream from the confluence of the rivers Tees and Skerne, this area has been liable to serious flood damage but recent measures have reduced the impact of rising river levels.

166   An ink and water-colour illustration entitled 'On Croft Bridge 1816' with the caption … 'Then the postboys spurned their horses, Ah there's nothing in the blood and bone, And they dashed as though crazed past the gateman amazed, At the chaise with four wheels bar none.' The page appeared in *Family Annals by road and rail by flood and field* published by Samuel Tuke Richardson of Darlington and Piercebridge.

167   A view of riverside property at Croft on a postcard dated 1909. Until recent flood relief schemes were completed, low-lying land on both sides of the river was subject to serious flooding.

168 The interior of Croft Church has reminders of Lewis Carroll's early days at Croft where his father (Rev. Dodgson) was rector but its dominant feature is the Milbanke pew. Measuring about fifteen feet in length, it is supported on oak pillars giving access from floor level. The ornate tomb in the background is for a member of the Milbanke family who lived at nearby Halnaby Hall.

169 Croft's earliest spa, now a farm building, dates from 1669 but after the opening of another spa, close to Croft Bridge in 1827, visitors flocked to the village in search of health-giving treatment. A pump room and suite of baths were built over the spring and by 1837 some 800 clients were taking regular baths in the water from sulphur magnesium and chalybeate springs. The boom period was short-lived and by 1841 the number of people visiting the spas at Croft was already in decline. This postcard dates from the early 1900s and the writer reports, 'We are benefiting from a health point of view but my old trouble persistently bothers me'.

170 A quiet day at Middleton One Row in 1913. Life in this village overlooking the Tees had been revolutionised by the development of a spa—a little distance upstream—and the arrival of the Stockton-Darlington railway in 1825. Until the 1960s this location was still a popular day trip for Darlington people.

171 *Dinsdale Spa Hotel* situated close to the river Tees a short distance upstream from Middleton One Row. In 1789 William Henry Lambton's workmen had drilled into a sulphur spring during exploration for coal at this place and bathing facilities were installed during the 1790s. New baths were completed in 1824 and during the late 1820s much of Middleton One Row was updated to cater for the increasing number of visitors. Many of these health-seekers arrived by rail at Dinsdale station and then travelled the short distance to Middleton by coach.

172 Family groups on the wide riverside walk leading to woodland upstream from Middleton One Row. During the late 1820s Lord Durham, son of Lord Lambton, built the large hotel on high ground above the bath house. Design work was carried out by Ignatius Bonomi and the completed building had over seventy well-furnished apartments. By the 1850s the spa's popularity had faded and the former hotel became a centre for 'a limited number of the higher and middle classes whose state of mind requires seclusion and medical treatment'.

173 An Edwardian postcard showing the original unofficial Darlington coat of arms which was in use from last century. The town did not have official arms granted by the College of Arms until May 1960. In spite of this the old arms was in constant use on transport, uniforms, lamp standards etc.

FLOREAT INDUSTRIA

DARLINGTON.

174 One of the little-known peaceful and secluded places in Darlington town centre is the Quaker burial ground behind the Friends' Meeting House in Skinnergate. Here are the simple, uniform headstones which mark the graves of numerous notable Quakers who played such an important role in the development of Darlington.

Bibliography

Books

Chilton, J. Douglas, O.B.E., *Jottings Over a Lifetime in and around Darlington* (1981)
Dean, D. & S.C., *Darlington in the 1930s and 1940s* (1984)
Dean, S.C. & Clough, U.M., *Darlington As It Was* (1974)
Flynn, G.J., *Darlington in Old Photographs* (1989)
Flynn, G.J., *Darlington in Old Photographs: A Second Selection* (1992)
Flynn, G.J., *Darlington in Old Picture Postcards* (1983)
Flynn, G.J., *Darlington in Old Picture Postcards*, volume 2 (1983)
Pevsner, N., *The Buildings of England: County Durham* (1983)
Thorold, H., *County Durham* (Shell Guide) (1980)

Local guides and monographs

Alan, Godfrey, *Maps: Darlington 1898 and Darlington South 1898*
Chapman, V., *Around Darlington in Old Photographs* (1990)
'Darlington Walkabout', *Borough of Darlington publication* (1975)
'Darlington & District', *Darlington District Civic Society* (1975)

Articles

Darlington and Stockton Times, Memory Lane Series
Darlington and Stockton Times, Various articles
Northern Echo, Various articles

Miscellaneous

A walk around historic Darlington published by Darlington Public Library (1974)
'Darlington Market Place Archaeological Excavations 1994', *University of Durham Archaeological Services* published by Darlington Borough Council (1996)

Index

Roman numerals refer to pages in the introduction, and arabic numerals to individual illustrations.

Ambulance service, 90
Anglian cemetery, ix
Anne, H.R.H. Princess, xvi
Aycliffe, 161

Bank Top Railway Station, 53, 56, 132
Barmpton Hall, 123
Barningham Church, 110
Beatrice, Princess, 120
Beaumont Street, 115
Bedford Street, 52
Belah Viaduct, xiii
Bell, William, xiii, 52
Bennet House, xvi
Blackett's, 110
Blackwell, 129, 130
Blackwellgate, xi, xii, 42, 45
Boer War celebrations, 3
Boldon Book, x
Bondgate, x, xii, 8, 37, 38, 39, 41
Bondgate Methodist Church, 76
Bonomi, Ignatius, xiii, 172
Boot and Shoe Hotel, 4, 34
Borough Hotel, 10
Botcherby, Robert, 71
Bradford brothers: xiv; Roland Boys, xiv; R.N. Lieutenant Commander George Nicholson, xiv
Broken Scar, xv
Bronze Age, ix
Brougham carriage, 131
Buck's Close, xv
Buckton's Yard, xiv
Bull, Wynd, xvi, 40
Bulmer's Stone, xiv, 36
Bulmer, Willie, xiv, 36

Calvert, Phyllis, xvi
Cambrai, xiv
Cardwell family, 157
Carmel Road, 128
Carroll, Lewis, 168
Charles II, King, xv
Chester, xv

Church Lane, 29
Civic Theatre, 82
Clark, Marjorie, 162
Clark's Yard, xiv
Cleveland Terrace, 68
Cockerton, xvi, 160
Colling, Charles, 124
Colling Shorthorn Memorial Challenge Cup, 125
Conyers Chapel, Sockburn, 154, 155, 156
Conyers, Sir John, 156
Cooper, Tommy, xv
Co-operation Day (1930), 118
Co-operative Society: 100, 103, 104, 105; Bakery Department delivery van, 102
Cornmill Shopping Centre, xvi, 27
Court Cinema, 51
Croft, 167
Croft Bridge, 156, 164
Croft Church, 168
Croft Spa, 169
Croft Spa Hotel, 165
Cromwell: Oliver, xv; Richard, xv
Crown Street, xiv, xvi

Darlington (Eastbourne) Allotments Ltd., 87
Darlington Amateur Operatic Society, xvi
Darlington Civic Theatre, xvi
Darlington Coat of Arms, 173
Darlington Corporation Light Railway, 147, 148
Darlington Forge: 107; Company Band, 109
Darlington Quoits Club, 96
Darlington Show (1920), 116
Darlington and Teesdale Naturalist Field Club, 89
Deanery, x
Dent, Joseph William, 116
Dinsdale rectory, 149

Dinsdale Spa Hotel, 171
Distel, Sacha, xvi
Dobbin, John, x
Dodd, Ken, xvi
Dolphin Centre, xvi
Drinking fountain, 65, 66
Durham, Lord, 172

Eanbald, Archbishop of York, 154, 155
Edward VII, King, 114
Edwin of Northumbria, ix
Elizabethan period, xv
Elizabeth I, Queen, xi
Elm Ridge, xii
Etty's steam printing works, 31
Eugenie, Princess, 120

Fawbert, 'Geordie', 95
Feethams, x, 54
Fighting Cocks, 138, 163
Fonteyn, Dame Margot, xvi
Forde, Florrie, xv
Fothergill, Dr. Algernon, 92
Fowler, John, 63
Fox's oriental café and creamery, 106
Friends Meeting House, Skinnergate, 174
Friends' Yard, xiv
Fry, Theodore, xii

Gallon's Ltd., 85
Grainey Hill Cottage, xiv
Grammar School, xi, 78
Grange Hotel, 64
Grange Road Baptist Chapel, 75
Great North Road, 12, 161
Greenbank Estate, ix
Greenbank Hospital, xii, 124

Halnaby Hall, 168
Harrowgate Hill, 84
Hat and Feathers, xvi, 4
Hatfield, Bishop, xi
Haughton le Skerne, xvi

Havelock-Allan, Sir Henry, x, xiv
Higbald of Lindisfarne, 154, 155
High Coniscliffe, 159
High Row, xii, 8-17, 21
Hinge, Teddy, xv
Hippodrome, xv
Holy Trinity Church, xiv
Horse fair, 38
Horse market, x
Hoskins, George Gordon, xi, xii
Houndgate, xi, 40
Hummersknott, xiii
Hundens Lane Isolation Hospital, xii

Indian Mutiny, xiv
Interregnum, xv
Iron Age, ix
Italian musicians, 149

Jenkins, Rev. William, 76

Ketton Hall, 123, 124
King's Head Hotel, 10, 12, 18, 20, 23, 37, 106

Lambton, William Henry, 171
Lauder, Harry, xv
Laye, Evelyn, xv
Lee, Sir William, 71
Liberal and Unionist Club, 77
Library, 72, 73
Linen industry, 36
Locomotion No.1, xiii, 136
London, xv
Low Coniscliffe, 157
Low Dinsdale, 150, 151, 153
Luck, Richard, x
Lucknow, x

Magnet Bowl, 73
Marshall, Robert, xi
Mechanics' Institute, xiv, 51
Mechanics' Yard, xiv, 44
Memorial Hospital, xii
Merrybent Railway Bridge, 157
Metcalfe, Ivy, 117
Methodist New Connexion Church, 56
Middleton One Row, 170, 171, 172
Middleton St George, ix
Middleton St George Ironworks, 138
Milbanke pew (Croft Church), 168
Military Cross, xiv

Model Dairy, 101
Monument Rooms, 19
Morritt, Thomas, 98
Mowden Hall, xiii, 70
Murphy, Michael, xiv, xv

Nag's Head Inn, 28, 29
Nathupur, xiv
Neasham, ix
'New Jerusalem', xiv
North Cemetery, xv
North Eastern Railway: xiii, 88;
    Locomotive works, 141, 142
Northgate, xi, xii, xvi, 8, 9, 36, 47, 48, 50
Northgate Lodge, xiii
North Lodge Park, 59, 60
North Road Station, xiii, 132, 139

Operatic Society, 83

Pall Mall Gazette, xiv
Parkgate, 53
Paulinus, ix
Pavlova, xv
Pease, Edward, xii, xiv
Pease: Edward Lucas, xiii;
    Henry, xii, 69; John, xii; John
    Beaumont, xiii; Joseph, xiii;
    Joseph (statue), 10, 13, 23
Pease's Mill, 8, 32, 73
Pepi, Signor Rino, xv
Piercebridge, ix, 158
Pierremont, 69
Prebend Row, 23
Pritchett, J.P., xiv, 74
Puiset, Hugh de, ix, x
Punch Bowl Inn, 127, 128

Quaker burial ground, 174

Railway Workers' Institute, 140
Redgrave, Sir Michael, xvi
Richardson, Samuel Tuke, 166
Richmond, xv
Richmond, Sid, 119
Roberts, Earl, 1
Robey, George, xv
Ropery Yard, 30

St Cuthbert's Church, xiv, xvi, 2
St Edwin's Church, 47
St John's Church, 53
St John's Church, Dinsdale, 150
St Mary's Church, Piercebridge, 158

St Paul's football team, 97
Saltburn Improvement Committee, xiv
Saltyard, 76
Scotch Corner Inn, 162
Shakespeare, William, xv
Skerne railway bridge, xiii, 137
Skinnergate, xi, xiv, 51
Smith & Son, W.H., 7
Snaith, R.T., 93, 94, 99, 110
Sockburn, 154, 155
South African War Memorial, 1
Southend, 64
South Park, 61
Speedwell Temperance Hotel, 56
Stead, W.T., xiv
Steam locomotive No. 62768, 146
Stephenson, 132
Stockton & Darlington Railway, xiii, 133, 134, 135, 136, 137, 138, 139, 144, 163, 170
Stockton on Tees, xi, xv
Stone Bridge, 1, 30, 32
Styr, ix
Sunday School Teachers' Conference, 113
Teacher Training College, 79, 80
Technical College, xiv, 36, 77
Tees Cottage pumping station, xv
Tetley, S., and Sons Ltd., 99
Theatre Royal, xv
Thorn's Theatre, xv
Three Tuns, 98
'Tiny Tim', 108
Titanic disaster, xiv
Tod, Peter, xvi
Trolley buses, 50
Tubwell Row, xvi, 24, 25, 26, 27, 28
Tutin, Dorothy, xvi

Vane Terrace, xi
Vaughan, Frankie, xv
Victoria Cross, xiv, xv
Victoria Road, 52, 54, 55, 56

Wallace, Nellie, xv
Waterhouse, Alfred, xii, xiii, 9
Whessoe Ltd., 91
Williamson, Faulkner Brown, xvi
'Woodlands', 71

Yards, 51
York, xv
Zeebrugge, xiv